# ZOMBIES

VS.

# ALIENS

**Disclaimer:**

The creatures in this book are not real. They are from myths. They are fun to imagine. Read the 45th Parallel Press series Magic, Myth, and Mystery to learn more about them.

45TH PARALLEL PRESS

Published in the United States of America by Cherry Lake Publishing
Ann Arbor, Michigan
www.cherrylakepublishing.com

Reading Adviser: Marla Conn, MS, Ed., Literacy specialist, Read-Ability Inc.
Book Designer: Melinda Millward

Photo Credits: © tsuneomp/Shutterstock.com, back cover, cover, 5, 16; © Borkin Vadim/Shutterstock.com, 6; © Ronald Sumners/Shutterstock.com, 9; © inhauscreative/istockphoto.com, 10; © Louella938/Shutterstock.com, 12; © Nyord/Shutterstock.com, 15; © 3000ad/Shutterstock.com, 19; © GraphicsRF/Shutterstock.com, 19, 20; © vectortatu/Shutterstock.com, 20; © Firstear/Shutterstock.com, 21; © Fer Gregory/Shutterstock.com, 23; © Dualororua/Shutterstock.com, 24; © Sebastian Kaulitzki/Shutterstock.com, 25; © stockcreations/Shutterstock.com, 25; © NASA images/Shutterstock.com, 27; © gremlin/istockphoto.com, 29

Graphic Element Credits: © studiostoks/Shutterstock.com, back cover, multiple interior pages; © infostocker/Shutterstock.com, back cover, multiple interior pages; © mxbfilms/Shutterstock.com, front cover; © MF production/Shutterstock.com, front cover, multiple interior pages; © AldanNi/Shutterstock.com, front cover, multiple interior pages; © Andrii Symonenko/Shutterstock.com, front cover, multiple interior pages; © acidmit/Shutterstock.com, front cover, multiple interior pages; © manop/Shutterstock.com, multiple interior pages; © Lina Kalina/Shutterstock.com, multiple interior pages; © mejorana/Shutterstock.com, multiple interior pages; © NoraVector/Shutterstock.com, multiple interior pages; © Smirnov Viacheslav/Shutterstock.com, multiple interior pages; © Piotr Urakau/Shutterstock.com, multiple interior pages; © IMOGI graphics/Shutterstock.com, multiple interior pages; © jirawat phueksriphan/Shutterstock.com, multiple interior pages



**45th Parallel Press** is an imprint of Cherry Lake Publishing.

Library of Congress Cataloging-in-Publication Data

Names: Loh-Hagan, Virginia, author.
Title: Zombies vs. aliens / by Virginia Loh-Hagan.
Description: Ann Arbor, Michigan : Cherry Lake Publishing, [2020] | Series: Battle royale: lethal warriors | Includes bibliographical references and index.
Identifiers: LCCN 2019032885 (print) | LCCN 2019032886 (ebook) | ISBN 9781534159372 (hardcover) | ISBN 9781534161672 (paperback) | ISBN 9781534160521 (pdf) | ISBN 9781534162822 (ebook)
Subjects: LCSH: Zombies–Juvenile literature. | Extraterrestrial beings–Juvenile literature.
Classification: LCC GR581 .L65 2020 (print) | LCC GR581 (ebook) | DDC 398.21–dc23
LC record available at https://lccn.loc.gov/2019032885
LC ebook record available at https://lccn.loc.gov/2019032886

Printed in the United States of America
Corporate Graphics

## About the Author

Dr. Virginia Loh-Hagan is an author, university professor, and former classroom teacher. She loves watching zombie and alien movies. She loves reading science fiction. She lives in San Diego with her very tall husband and very naughty dogs. To learn more about her, visit www.virginialoh.com.

# Table of Contents

# Introduction

Imagine a battle between zombies and aliens. Who would win? Who would lose?

Enter the world of *Battle Royale: Lethal* **Warriors**! Warriors are fighters. This is a fight to the death! The last team standing is the **victor**! Victors are winners. They get to live.

**Opponents** are fighters who compete against each other. They challenge each other. They fight with everything they've got. They use weapons. They use their special skills. They use their powers.

They're not fighting for prizes. They're not fighting for honor. They're fighting for their lives. Victory is their only option.

Let the games begin!

VS.

# ZOMBIES

Zombie stories started in West Africa. It all began with voodoo. Voodoo is a religion. It uses folk magic.

Zombies are **undead** creatures. Zombies are people who died. They were brought back to life. They don't have free will. They can't think. They have **decomposing** bodies. Their bodies break down. Their skin slowly rots. Their muscles are damaged. They smell really bad. They limp. They move slowly. They're clumsy. They walk in a zigzag. They hang their heads. They moan. They groan. They have brain damage. They're not smart. But they're focused. They destroy. They eat. Nothing stops them.

There are different types of zombies. Walkers are the most common. Runners are the most dangerous. They can run. They're new zombies. Crawlers don't have legs. Their lower bodies were chopped off. They crawl. They bite ankles. Spitters spit poison. They can spit far. Their spit burns. Boneys are what zombies become. Their flesh has completely rotted off. They're old zombies.

Zombies are scary. They eat brains. They attack. They bite. They **infect** others. Infect means to spread sickness. They turn humans into zombies. There is no cure. Once a person is bitten, that person is doomed. A zombie **apocalypse** is when zombies take over. Zombies attack humans. They take over cities.

Zombies are most powerful when first infected. They can still move like humans.

Zombies are stronger than humans. They never get tired. They never sleep. They don't feel pain. They live without food or water. They can smell well. They can hear well. They like noise. They go to loud noises.

They attack in **hordes**. Hordes are zombie groups. Their strength is in numbers. They trap humans. They attack from all sides. Their infection spreads quickly. Their infection spreads far. Then, they eat.

Zombies have weaknesses. They're slower than humans. They can't use tools. They can't heal. Zombies can be killed by damaging their brains. They can be killed by cutting off their heads. Fires can also kill zombies.

# FUN FACTS ABOUT ZOMBIES

- October 8 is World Zombie Day. Many cities celebrate. People dress as zombies. They walk in a parade. It first started in 2006. It first started in Pittsburgh, Pennsylvania. This is where the 1978 movie *Dawn of the Dead* was filmed.

- George Washington was almost the first "zombie president" of the United States. He died in 1799. His dead body was on ice for 3 days. William Thornton was a doctor. He wanted to bring Washington back to life. He wanted to pump air into Washington's lungs. He wanted to give Washington lamb's blood. Washington's family denied Thornton's idea.

- Zombies are mentioned in *Epic of Gilgamesh*. This book is over 5,000 years old. It features an angry goddess. The goddess threatens to bring the dead back to eat the living.

# ALIENS

In real life, we know very little about aliens.

Aliens are beings from outer space. Some people say they had close **encounters** with aliens. Encounters are meetings. There are different types of close encounters. There are sightings of a **UFO**. This stands for unidentified flying object. A UFO is a spaceship. People can either see it with their eyes or take a photo. Sometimes direct contact is made. Humans make contact with aliens. Sometimes they are **abducted**. To abduct means to kidnap.

Grey aliens are the most common aliens. They are gray. They're **humanoids**. Humanoids are creatures that are shaped like humans. Grey aliens have big heads. They have large, black eyes. Their eyes are shaped like almonds. Grey aliens have a pair of small slits for a nose. They have a small mouth. They have long, skinny arms and legs. Grey aliens kidnap humans. They do tests on humans.

There are many other aliens. Some aliens look like monsters. They may have claws. They may have **fangs** or sharp teeth. They may have many eyes. They may have tails. They may have **tentacles**. Tentacles are long, moving arms.

Some aliens look like reptiles.

Aliens have a lot of different powers. Some aliens are super strong. Some are really fast. Some can read and control minds. Some can move things with their mind. Some can heal themselves. Some can change shapes. Some can become invisible. Some are **predators** with super senses. Predators are hunters.

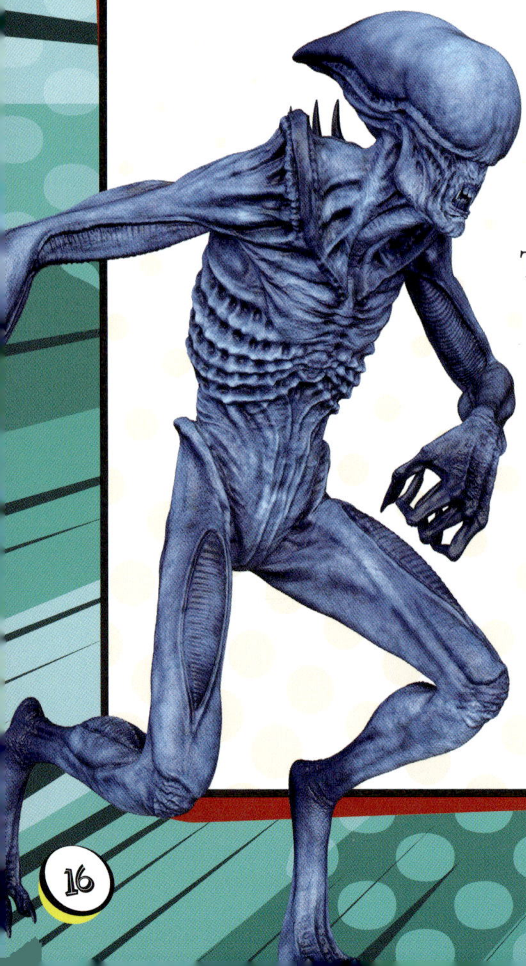

Some aliens are super smart. They're smarter than humans. They have better technology. They've mastered space travel. Their spaceships have super computers.

Aliens may have several weaknesses. Some aliens can be killed by fire, water, or electricity. Some aliens may die from human sicknesses.

# FUN FACTS ABOUT ALIENS

- Roswell is in New Mexico. It's home to military bases. Roswell is famous for its close encounters. It's known as "ground zero" for UFO research. Ground zero means starting point. It's most famous for the 1947 UFO incident. Incident means event. People think a UFO crashed there.

- Betty and Barney Hill said aliens kidnapped them. They said they were taken to a UFO. This happened in 1961. They said the aliens had gray skin. They called them Greys. Some people think Greys and Roswell aliens are at Area 51. Area 51 is a Nevada air force base. It's believed to have top secret files. It's believed to have proof of aliens.

- Orson Welles had a radio show. He based it on a science-fiction book. The book is *War of the Worlds*. Welles told people aliens were invading Earth. Many people listened to the show. They believed him. This happened in 1938.

# CHOOSE YOUR BATTLEGROUND

Zombies and aliens are fierce fighters. They're well-matched. But they have different ways of fighting. So, choose your battleground carefully!

# Battleground #1: Sea

• Zombies can go in water. They don't need air. They won't drown. But they can't swim. The sea water would damage their bodies. Bodies rot faster in water. Fish would eat their decaying skin.

• Aliens are good space fighters. There are many similarities between space and the deep sea. There's not much air in either place. But some aliens are scared of water.

There are many different types of spaceships.

## Battleground #2: Land

- Zombies walk around land. They find places with lots of humans. They like hospitals. They like malls. They like cities. These are hot spots.

- Aliens fly in space. They land on ground. They learn to adapt to our air.

## Battleground #3: Mountains

- Zombies would have a hard time walking up mountains. They would fall down a lot. They're better on flat land. They would trip over rocks.

- Aliens are used to being high in the air. Mountains have thin air. The thin air wouldn't bother aliens.

# ARMED AND DANGEROUS: WEAPONS

**Zombies:** Zombies' best weapon is their teeth. They don't have working brains anymore. So, they don't think. Their jaw muscles have been turned off. They just bite all the time. A zombie bite is powerful. It's as strong as a trained attack dog's bite. This is over 3 times stronger than a normal human's bite. Zombies bite a lot. The flesh around their mouth is damaged. Most zombies only have teeth and jawbones left.

**Aliens:** A popular alien weapon is a ray gun. Ray guns fire beams. The beams are destructive energy. They look like light rays. They can be seen. They're hot. They cut things. They blow things up. They make things disappear. Ray guns make bright light. They make loud noises. They have different names. They've been called death rays, blasters, and zap guns. They're usually fastened on spaceships.

# FIGHT ON!

The battle begins! It's almost nighttime. Zombies are most active at night. Aliens can see in day or night. Zombies are walking around an open field. There's a fence around the field. This keeps the zombies in one place. A UFO lands. Zombies hear the spaceship noises. They go toward the UFO. Aliens walk out of their UFO.

## Move 1:

Aliens group up together. They put their backs against each other. They make sure no zombies can come behind them. They move forward as a group. They aim their weapons. Fireballs shoot out of their weapons. The fireballs hit the zombies.

Aliens are blamed for many things we can't explain.

## Move 2:

Zombies fall back. They stumble to the ground. They try to get up. They roll around on the ground. They put out the fires. There are burn marks on their bodies. But they're still moving. Their jaws keep biting.

## Move 3:

The aliens are confused. They wonder why the zombies don't die. More zombies walk toward the aliens. They make biting motions. Aliens can hear the zombies' teeth clash. Zombies try to bite the aliens. Aliens use special curved swords. They swing their swords. They cut zombies in half. But the zombies are still moving.

Feeding time can be dangerous. Zombies don't like sharing human brains.

# LIFE SOURCE: FOOD FOR BATTLE

**Zombies:** Offal are the organs of an animal used as food. Zombies eat offal. They eat brains. Human brains weigh about 3 pounds (1 kilogram). They're the fattiest organ in the body. About 60 percent of the brain consists of fats. The brain uses this fat to make cells. Humans have the largest brain-to-body ratio of any animal. The brain has a lot of blood vessels. If stretched out, the vessels would be 100,000 miles (160,934 kilometers) long.

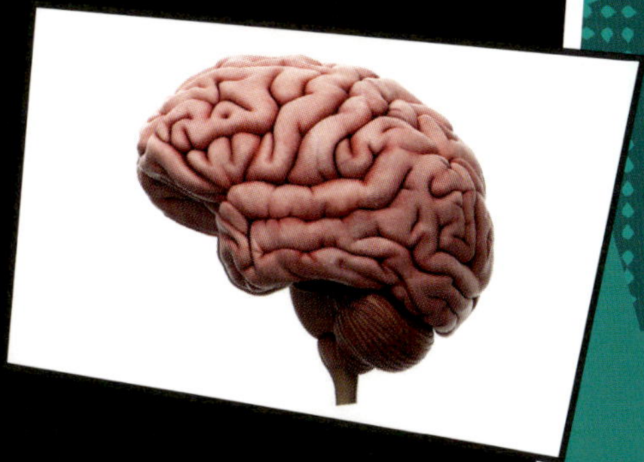

**Aliens:** It is said aliens eat humans. But aliens' bodies aren't made to eat humans. It would be hard for them to process meat. Plus, human blood has too much iron. Experts say aliens would prefer vegetables. Aliens eat to get energy. Vegetables give cleaner, purer, and lighter energy. Aliens could also take in energy through their body like plants.

## Move 4:

Zombies attack. It takes time for aliens to swing their curved swords. Zombies use that time. They bite at the aliens.

## Move 5:

One alien turns his finger into a sharp sword. He cuts off a zombie's head. He stabs another zombie in the head. The zombies stop biting. They stop moving. The aliens realize they need to attack zombie heads.

## Move 6:

Aliens don't act as a team. They act separately. One alien separates himself from the group. The zombies head toward the alien. They close in on the alien. They work as a horde.

Many scientists study space.
Some search for life outside of Earth.

# AND THE VICTOR IS . . .

*What are their next moves?*

*Who do you think would win?*

## Zombies could win if:

- They fight in cold weather. They like cold weather. The cold and snow keep zombies from rotting. They'll be able to fight longer when it's cold.
- They protect their brains. That's the only way they can die.

## Aliens could win if:

- They avoid getting trapped in small spaces. A horde could overtake them.
- They fight in their spaceship. Zombies can't fly. They can only stay on the ground.

More people believe in aliens than zombies.

## Zombies: Top Champion

Jason Voorhees is the main character in the *Friday the 13th* movies. He was born on Friday the 13th. He had a tough life. He almost drowned as a young child. He grows up in the woods by himself. He grows up and becomes a killer. He stalks and kills people. One day, he gets killed. But he comes back to life. He becomes an evil zombie. He wears a white hockey goalie mask. His face is really ugly. He has a lot of scars from stabbings, gunshots, and burns. He doesn't talk. He doesn't have a personality. But he does have superhuman strength. He's very strong. He can heal himself. He's hard to kill. He has a machete. Machetes are broad, heavy knives. But Jason has a weakness. He becomes helpless if trapped underwater. He also doesn't kill animals or children.

## Aliens: Top Champion

The Demogorgon is an alien monster in the Netflix show *Stranger Things*. It's inspired by a monster in the game *Dungeons & Dragons*. It comes from another world called the Upside Down. It passes through a crack in the gate in 1983. It kidnaps people. It takes them back to the Upside Down. It can travel between worlds whenever it wants. It's a humanoid. It's very large, tall, and thin. It has long, skinny arms and legs. It has sharp claws. It has slimy skin. It doesn't have facial features. The flesh on his face opens like a flower. The flesh petals open to show many sharp teeth. The Demogorgon has a large, open mouth. It's a predator. It's lured by blood. It growls and yells. It's violent. It's very strong. It can break walls. It can throw men around. It can heal itself. Its skin is bulletproof.

# Consider This!

## THINK ABOUT IT!

- How are zombies and aliens alike? How are they different? Are they more alike or different? Why do you think so?
- Read the 45th Parallel Press books about zombies and Roswell. What more did you learn about these creatures?
- What skills do you have to fight a zombie? What skills do you have to fight an alien?
- There are many movies and books about zombies and aliens. Make a list of the ones you have read or seen. Which one is your favorite? Why? How did the story change the myths about zombies and aliens?

## LEARN MORE!


- Halls, Kelly Milner, and Rick C. Spears (illustr.). *Alien Investigation: Searching for the Truth about UFOs and Aliens*. Minneapolis, MN: Millbrook Press, 2012.
- Loh-Hagan, Virginia. *Roswell*. Ann Arbor, MI: Cherry Lake Publishing, 2017.
- Loh-Hagan, Virginia. *Zombies*. Ann Arbor, MI: Cherry Lake Publishing, 2016.
- Owen, Ruth. *Zombies and Other Walking Dead*. New York, NY: Bearport Publishing, 2013.


## GLOSSARY

**abducted** (ab-DUHKT-id) kidnapped
**apocalypse** (uh-PAHK-uh-lips) the final destruction of the world
**decomposing** (dee-kuhm-POZE-ing) rotting
**encounters** (en-KOUN-turz) meetings or interactions
**fangs** (FANGZ) sharp, pointy teeth
**hordes** (HORDZ) groups
**humanoids** (HYOO-muh-noydz) creatures that are shaped like humans
**infect** (in-FEKT) to make others sick, to spread sickness
**opponents** (uh-POH-nuhnts) fighters who compete against each other
**predators** (PRED-uh-turz) hunters
**tentacles** (TEN-tuh-kuhlz) long, moving arms with suckers
**UFO** (YOO EF OH) unidentified flying object or spaceship
**undead** (uhn-DED) creatures who are dead but animated like vampires, zombies, and mummies
**victor** (VIK-tur) the winner
**warriors** (WOR-ee-urz) fighters

## INDEX